Hans Christian Andersen's

The Fir-Tree

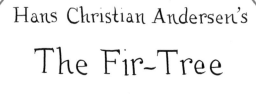

by Lilli Carré

!t
itbooks
AN IMPRINT OF HARPERCOLLINS PUBLISHERS

THE FIR-TREE. Copyright © 2009 by Lilli Carré. All rights reserved. Printed in
China. No part of this book may be used or reproduced in any manner whatsoever
without written permission except in the case of brief quotations embodied in
critical articles and reviews. For information address HarperCollins Publishers,
10 East 53rd Street, New York, NY 10022.

HarperCollins books may be purchased for educational, business, or sales
promotional use. For information please write: Special Markets Department,
HarperCollins Publishers, 10 East 53rd Street, New York, NY 10022.

FIRST EDITION

ISBN 978-0-06-178236-7

09   10   11   12   13   10   9   8   7   6   5   4   3   2   1

Far down in the forest, where the warm sun and fresh air made a sweet resting place,

grew a pretty little fir-tree

and yet it was not happy; it wished so much to be tall like its companions — the pines and firs which grew around it. The sun shone, and the soft air fluttered its leaves, and the little peasant children passed by, prattling merrily, but the fir-tree heeded them not.

Sometimes the children would bring a large basket of raspberries or strawberries, wreathed in straw, and seat themselves near the fir-tree, and say,

Is it not a pretty little tree?

which made it feel more unhappy than before.

And yet all this while the tree grew a notch or joint taller every year;

for by the number of joints in the stem of a fir-tree we can discover its age.

Still, as it grew, it complained,

Oh! How I wish I were as tall as the other trees, then I would spread out my branches on every side, and my top would overlook the wide world.

I should have the birds building their nests on my boughs, and when the wind blew, I should bow with stately dignity like my tall companions.

The tree was so discontented that it took no pleasure in the warm sunshine, the birds, or the rosy clouds that floated over it morning and evening.

Sometimes, in winter, when the snow lay white and glittering on the ground, a hare would come springing along, and jump right over the little tree; and then how mortified it would feel!

Two winters passed,

and when the third arrived,
the tree had grown so tall
that the hare was obliged
to run around it.

Yet it remained unsatisfied,
and would exclaim,

Oh, if I could but keep
on growing tall and old!
There is nothing else worth
caring for in the world!

In the autumn, as usual,
the woodcutters came
and cut down
several
of the
tallest
trees,

and the young fir-tree,
which was now grown to its
full height, shuddered as the
noble trees fell to the earth
with a crash.

After the branches were lopped off, the trunks looked so slender and bare that they could scarcely be recognized.

Then they were placed upon wagons, and drawn by horses out of the forest. Where were they going? What would become of them?

The young fir-tree wished
very much to know; so in
the spring, when the
swallows and the
storks came,
it asked,

Do you know where those trees were taken?

Did you meet them?

The swallows
knew nothing,
but the stork,
after a little reflection,
nodded his head, and said,

Yes, I think I do. I met several new ships when I
flew from Egypt, and they had fine masts that smelt
like fir. I think these must have been the trees;
I assure you they were stately, very stately.

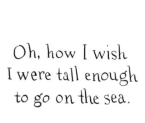

Oh, how I wish
I were tall enough
to go on the sea.

What is the sea,
and what does
it look like?

It would
take too much
time to explain.

Rejoice in
thy youth
said the
sunbeam.

Rejoice in thy fresh
growth, and the young
life that is in thee.

And the wind kissed the tree,
and the dew watered it with tears;
but the fir-tree regarded them not.

Christmastime drew near, and many young trees were cut down, some even smaller than the fir-tree, who enjoyed neither rest nor peace with longing to leave its forest home.

These young trees, which were chosen for their beauty, kept their branches, and were also laid on wagons and drawn by horses out of the forest.

Where are they going?
asked the fir-tree.

They are not taller than I am;
indeed, one is much less;
and why are the branches not cut off?

Where are they going?

We know,
we know.

We have looked in at
the windows of the houses
in the town, and we know
what is done with them.

They are dressed up in the most splendid manner. We have seen them standing in the middle of a warm room, and adorned with all sorts of beautiful things:

honey cakes

gilded apples

playthings

and many hundreds of wax tapers

"And then," asked the fir-tree, trembling through all its branches, "and then what happens?"

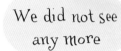
We did not see
any more

but this was
enough for us.

I wonder whether anything so brilliant will ever
happen to me. It would be much better than
crossing the sea. I long for it almost with pain.
Oh! when will Christmas be here? I am now
as tall and well grown as those which were
taken away last year.

Oh! that I were now laid on the wagon or standing in the warm room, with all that brightness and splendor around me! Something better and more beautiful is to come after, or the trees would not be so decked out. Yes, what follows will be grander and more splendid. What can it be? I am weary with longing. I scarcely know how I feel.

Rejoice with us
said the air and the sunlight.

Enjoy thine own bright
life in the fresh air.

But the tree would not rejoice, though
it grew taller every day; and, winter and
summer, its dark-green foliage might be seen
in the forest, while passersby would say,

What a
beautiful
tree!

A short time before Christmas, the discontented fir-tree was the first to fall.

As the axe cut through the stem, and divided the pith, the tree fell with a groan to the earth, conscious of pain and faintness,

and forgetting all its anticipations of happiness, in sorrow at leaving its home in the forest.

It knew that it should never
again see its dear old companions,
the trees, nor the little bushes
and many-colored flowers
that had grown by its side;
perhaps not even the birds.

Neither was the journey at all pleasant. The tree first recovered itself while being unpacked in the courtyard of a house, with several other trees; and it heard a man say,

We only want one, and this is the prettiest.

Then came two servants in grand livery, and carried the fir-tree into a large and beautiful apartment. On the walls hung pictures, and near the great stove stood great china vases, with lions on the lids.

There were rocking chairs,
silken sofas, large tables
covered with pictures, books,
and playthings

worth a great
deal of money

at least,
the children
said so.

Then the fir-tree was placed in a large tub,
full of sand; but green baize hung all around it,
so that no one could see it was a tub, and it
stood on a very handsome carpet.

How the fir-tree trembled!

What was going to happen to it now?

Some young ladies came, and the servants helped them to adorn the tree.

On one branch they hung little bags cut out of colored paper, and each bag was filled with sweet meats;

from other branches hung gilded apples and walnuts, as if they had grown there; and above, and all round, were hundreds of red, blue, and white tapers, which were fastened on the branches.

Dolls, exactly like real babies,
were placed under the green
leaves — the tree had never seen
such things before—

and at the very top was fastened
a glittering star, made of tinsel.
Oh, it was very beautiful!

"This evening," they all exclaimed,
"how bright it will be!"

Oh, that the evening were come and the tapers
lighted! Then I shall know what else is going
to happen. Will the trees of the forest come
to see me? I wonder if the sparrows will
peep in at the windows as they fly?
Shall I grow faster here, and keep on all
these ornaments summer and winter?

But guessing was of very little use;
it made its bark ache, and this pain
is as bad for a slender fir-tree,
as a headache is for us.

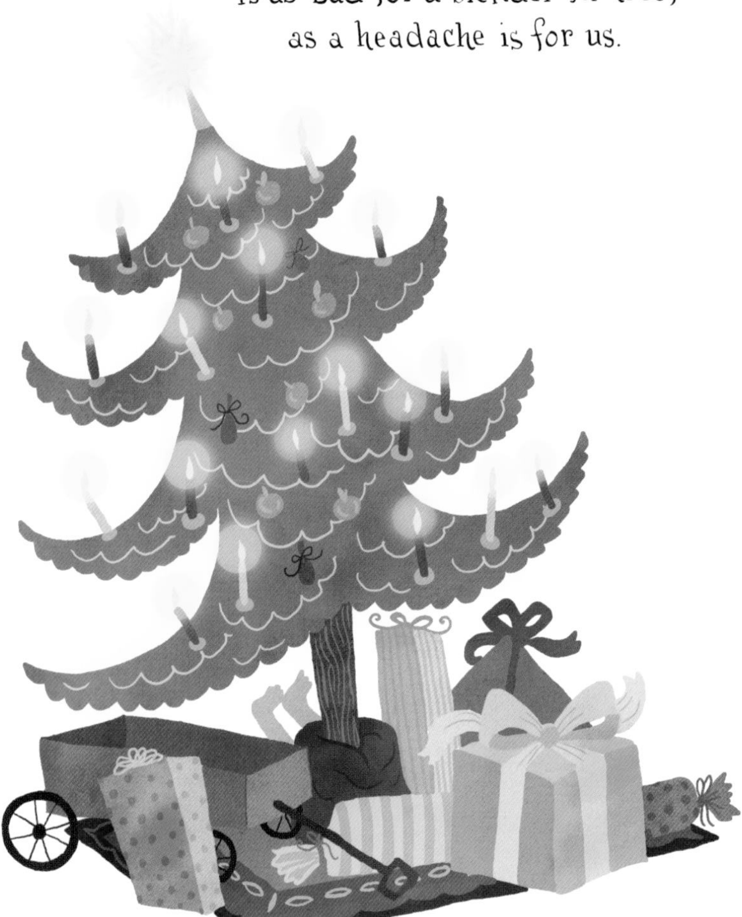

At last the tapers were lighted, and what
a glistening blaze of light the tree presented!

It trembled so with joy in all its branches
that one of the candles fell among the green
leaves and burnt some of them.

Help!

Help!

exclaimed
the young ladies,
but there was
no danger, for
they quickly
extinguished
the fire.

After this, the tree tried not to tremble at all,
though the fire frightened it; it was so anxious
not to hurt any of the beautiful ornaments,
even while their brilliancy dazzled it.

And now the folding doors were thrown
open, and a troop of children rushed in
as if they intended to upset the tree;

they were followed more silently
by their elders.

For a moment the little ones stood
silent with astonishment,

and then they shouted for joy,
till the room rang,

and they danced merrily round the tree,
while one present after another was
taken from it.

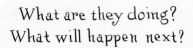

What are they doing?
What will happen next?

thought the fir.

At last the candles burnt down to the branches and were put out. Then the children received permission to plunder the tree.

Oh, how they rushed upon it, till the branches cracked, and had it not been fastened with the glistening star to the ceiling, it might have been thrown down.

The children then danced about with their
pretty toys, and no one noticed the tree,
except the children's maid, who came and
peeped among the branches to see if
an apple or a fig had been forgotten.

A story, a story

cried the children, pulling a little
fat man towards the tree.

Now we shall be in
the green shade, and the
tree will have the pleasure
of hearing also, but I shall
only relate one story; what
shall it be? Ivede-Avede, or
Humpty Dumpty, who fell
down stairs, but soon got
up again, and at last
married a princess.

Ivede-Avede

cried some.

Humpty
Dumpty

cried others,

and there was a fine shouting and crying out.
But the fir-tree remained quite still
and thought to itself,
"Shall I have anything to do with all this?"
but it had already amused them
as much as they wished.

Then the old man told them the story
of Humpty Dumpty, how he fell down
stairs, and was raised up again, and
married a princess. And the children
clapped their hands and cried,

Tell another
Tell another

for they wanted to hear the story of
Ivede-Avede, but they only had
Humpty Dumpty.

After this the fir-tree became quite silent
and thoughtful; never had the birds in the
forest told such tales as Humpty Dumpty,
who fell down the stairs, and yet
married a princess.

Ah! yes, so it happens in the world

thought the fir-tree; he believed
it all, because it was related
by such a nice man.

Ah! well, who knows? perhaps I may
fall down too, and marry a princess.

And he looked forward joyfully to the next
evening, expecting to be again decked out
with lights and playthings, gold and fruit.

Tomorrow I will not tremble.
I will enjoy all my splendor,
and I shall hear the story
of Humpty Dumpty again,
and perhaps Ivede-Avede.

And the tree remained quiet
and thoughtful all night.

In the morning the servants and the housemaid came in. "Now," thought the fir, "all my splendor is going to begin again."

But they dragged it out of the room and up stairs to the garret, and threw it on the floor, in a dark corner, where no daylight shone, and they left it.

What does this mean?
What am I to do here?
I can hear nothing
in a place like this.

And it had time enough to think,
for days and nights passed
and no one came near it

and when at last somebody did come,
it was only to put away large boxes
in a corner.

So the tree was completely hidden from sight as if it had never existed.

It is winter now.
The ground is hard and covered with snow so that people cannot plant me. I shall be sheltered here, I daresay, until spring comes. How thoughtful and kind everybody is to me! Still I wish this place were not so dark, as well as lonely, with not even a little hare to look at.

How pleasant it was out in the
forest while the snow lay on the
ground, when the hare would run
by, yes, and jump over me too,
although I did not like it then.

Oh! it is terribly lonely here.

squeak
squeak

said a little mouse, creeping cautiously towards the tree; then came another; and they both sniffed at the fir-tree and crept between the branches.

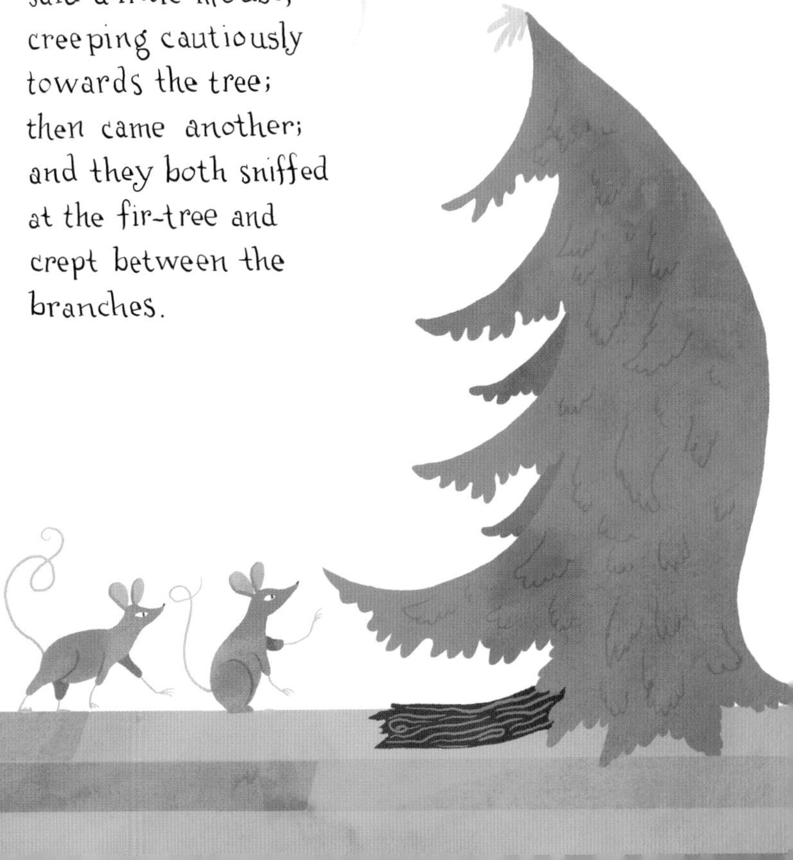

Oh, it is very cold,
or else we should be so
comfortable here, shouldn't we,
you old fir-tree?

I am not old.
There are many who
are older than I am.

Where do
you come
from?

And what
do you
know?

Have you seen the most beautiful places in the world, and can you tell us all about them?

And have you been in the storeroom, where cheeses lie on the shelf, and hams hang from the ceiling? One can run about on tallow candles there, and go in thin and come out fat.

I know nothing of that place, but I know the wood where the sun shines and the birds sing.

And then the tree told the little mice all about its youth. They had never heard such an account in their lives; and after they had listened to it attentively, they said,

What a number of things you have seen. You must have been very happy.

Happy!

exclaimed the fir-tree, and then as it reflected upon what it had been telling them, it said,

Ah, yes! After all, those were the happy days.

But then it went on and related all about Christmas Eve, and how it had been dressed up with cakes and lights.

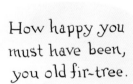

How happy you must have been, you old fir-tree.

And the next night four other mice came with them to hear what the tree had to tell.

The more it talked the more it remembered,
and then it thought to itself,

Those were happy days, but they
may come again. Humpty Dumpty
fell down stairs, and yet he married
the princess; perhaps I may
marry a princess too.

And the fir-tree thought of the pretty little
birch-tree that grew in the forest,
which was to it a real beautiful princess.

Who is Humpty
Dumpty?

asked the little mice.
And then the fir-tree related
the whole story; it could remember
every single word, and the little mice
were so delighted with it that
they were ready to jump
to the top of the tree.

The next night a great many more mice
made their appearance, and on Sunday
two rats came with them;
but they said,

It was not a
pretty story
at all

and the little mice were
very sorry, for it made them
also think less of it.

Do you know only one story?
Only one. I heard it on the happiest evening of my life; but I did not know I was so happy at the time.
We think it is a very miserable story. Don't you know any story about bacon, or tallow in the storeroom?

No

replied the tree.

Many thanks
to you, then

replied the rats,
and they marched off.

The little mice also crept away after this,
and the tree sighed, and said,

It was
very pleasant
when the merry little
mice sat round me and
listened while I talked.
Now that is all passed
too. However, I shall
consider myself happy
when someone comes
to take me out of
this place.

But would this ever happen?
Yes; one morning people came to clear out
the garret, the boxes were packed away,
and the tree was pulled out of the corner
and thrown roughly on the garret floor.

Then the servant dragged it out upon the staircase where the daylight shone.

Now my life is beginning again!

said the tree, rejoicing in the sunlight and the fresh air.

Then it was carried downstairs and taken into the courtyard so quickly that it forgot to think of itself, and could only look about, there was so much to see.

The court was close to a garden, where everything looked blooming. Fresh and fragrant roses hung over the little palings. The linden-trees were in blossom; while the swallows flew here and there, crying,

twit, twit, twit, my mate is coming

but it was not the fir-tree they meant.

Now I shall live!

cried the tree, joyfully
spreading out its branches.

But alas! they were all withered and yellow,
and it lay in a corner among weeds and
nettles. The star of gold paper still
stuck in the top of the tree and
glittered in the sunshine.

In the same courtyard were playing
two of the merry children who had danced
round the tree at Christmas, and had been
so happy. The youngest saw the gilded
star, and ran and pulled it off the tree.

Look what is sticking to the
ugly old fir-tree

said the child, treading on the
branches till they crackled
under his boots.

And the tree saw all the bright flowers in the garden, and then looked at itself, and wished it had remained in the dark corner of the garret. It thought of its fresh youth in the forest, of the merry Christmas evening, and of the little mice who had listened to the story of Humpty Dumpty.

Past! Past! Oh, had I but enjoyed myself while I could have done so! But now it is too late.

Then a lad came and chopped the tree into small pieces, till a large bundle lay in a heap on the ground.

The pieces were placed in a fire under the copper, and they quickly blazed up brightly, while the tree sighed so deeply that each sigh was like a pistol shot.

Pop!

Then the children, who were at play, came and seated themselves in front of the fire, and looked at it and cried, Pop!

Pop!

But at each "pop," which was a deep sigh,
the tree was thinking of a summer day in
the forest, and of Christmas evening, and
of Humpty Dumpty, the only story it
had ever heard or knew how to relate,
till at last it was consumed.

The boys still played in the garden,
and the youngest wore the golden star
on his breast, with which the tree
had been adorned during the
happiest evening of its existence.

Now all was past;
the tree's life was past,
and this story also—
for all stories must come
to an end at last.